My wonder weeks journal

Best. Journal. Ever.

By **Me** and **Xaviera Plas**

KW
PUBLISHING

My Wonder Weeks Journal

Copyright © Kiddy World Publishing
Written by: Me & Xaviera Plas
Concept Creation by: Anita Peereboom
Internal Design by: Andrei Andras
Illustrations: Hetty van de Rijt, Vladimir Schmeisser
Cover design by: Femke den Hertog

Kiddy World Publishing
Van Pallandtstraat 63
6814 GN Arnhem
The Netherlands
www.thewonderweeks.com

My Wonder Weeks Journal

Congratulations! You just made yourself the author of the best, most treasured book ever. This is a book that shows how your baby developed during the first 20 months of his/her life.

Write as you and your baby experience each magical leap in this journal. The questions will help you to observe the typical traits of each Wonder Week. Don't know the answer to a question right away? Just take your time to look at this aspect of your baby's development before answering. You will see that this will become the best, most special book you will ever write.

Collect and create the best of each leap at the Scrapbook page. Be as creative as you want! Just stick all your special memorabilia on these pages. It might be a receipt of the latte you drank at that special little café where the waiters always compliment your baby, the label of the bear that was interesting to your baby this leap, or a lipstick kiss of grandma who, just like with every leap, kissed your baby all over. It's these little memories that make a big difference later on!

We would LOVE to see what you created! Please share your Scrapbook pages or any other pages with us! Mail them, post them, tweet them, or pin them!

Have fun creating the best journal ever!

Love,
Xaviera

Date of birth: ....
Due date: ....

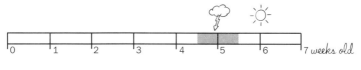

Leap 1 date ....

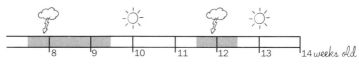

Leap 2 date ....   Leap 3 date ....

Leap 4 date ....

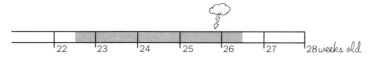

Leap 5 date ....

Leap 6 date ....

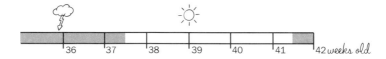

Leap 7 date ....

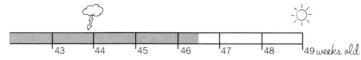

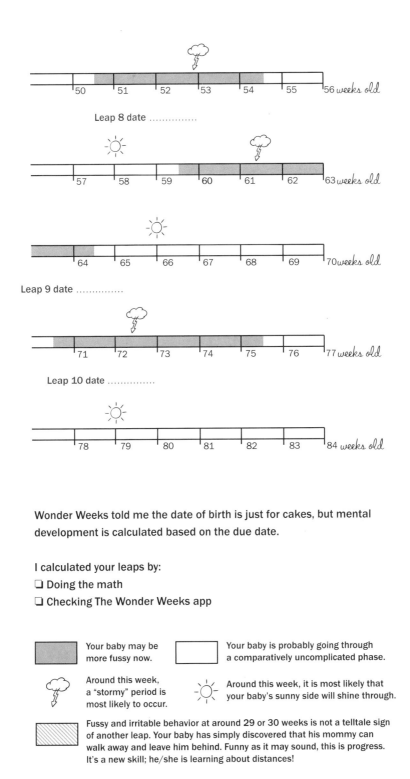

50 51 52 53 54 55 56 weeks old

Leap 8 date ....

57 58 59 60 61 62 63 weeks old

64 65 66 67 68 69 70 weeks old

Leap 9 date ....

71 72 73 74 75 76 77 weeks old

Leap 10 date ....

78 79 80 81 82 83 84 weeks old

Wonder Weeks told me the date of birth is just for cakes, but mental development is calculated based on the due date.

I calculated your leaps by:
❑ Doing the math
❑ Checking The Wonder Weeks app

Your baby may be more fussy now.

Your baby is probably going through a comparatively uncomplicated phase.

Around this week, a "stormy" period is most likely to occur.

Around this week, it is most likely that your baby's sunny side will shine through.

Fussy and irritable behavior at around 29 or 30 weeks is not a telltale sign of another leap. Your baby has simply discovered that his mommy can walk away and leave him behind. Funny as it may sound, this is progress. It's a new skill; he/she is learning about distances!

The World of
Changing
Sensations

Suddenly you understand
the world is not one thing.

This
Wonder Week's fussy signs

Date: ....

You are now making your first leap. I noticed this because you:

....

....

....

On a scale of fussiness, I would say this leap is a:

☀— 1   2   3   4   5   6   7   8   9   10 ⛈

The top three ways to soothe you were:

1. ....

2. ....

3. ....

This is how I felt:

....

....

....

On a scale of feeling ❏ desperate / ❏ insecure / ❏ .... I felt:

☀— 1   2   3   4   5   6   7   8   9   10 ⛈

Your
three C's

The difference in:

Clinginess:

....

....

Crying:

....

....

Crankiness:

....

....

And don't forget about the difference in:

Sleeping:

....

....

Drinking:

....

....

> Although making a leap is not that easy, it's actually a sign that progress is on its way. The next pages will reveal what you have learned from the first leap you made.

Your exploration

Yeah! You made your first leap in your mental development. This is how you explored the world of Changing Sensations.

It's clear that you perceive the world in a different way than before the leap. This is what I noticed:

....
....
....
....
....
....
....
....
....
....
....
....
....
....
....
....
....

Your emotions

I can see you show your emotions in a different way:

....
....
....
....
....

Your smile:

....
....
....
....
....

These are some physical changes that I noticed in regards to the little things like breathing, startling, trembling, crying, burping, and vomiting:

....
....
....
....
....

Your
eyes

These are some pictures of things you like to look at. They are all simple little things, but they mean the world to you.

....

....

....

....

....

....

....

....

....

....

....

....

❑ You like to look and study the same things over and over again
❑ You get bored easily, and you want to see new things every time
❑ You look at objects longer and with more interest now
❑ The brighter the objects, the more interesting they are

Your
sounds & touches

You react to sounds differently now than before in a way that:

....
....
....

These sounds appeal to you most:

....
....
....

These sounds scared you:

....
....
....

The little noises you now make are:

....
....
....

These are the ways you like to be touched now:

....
....
....

Your
special activities

Everybody has their own personal activities they like to do with you!

These things you like to do most with:

....
....
....
....

With .... your most loved activities are:

....
....
....
....

With .... you like to:

....
....
....
....

This is how you "tell" us you want a small break from all these activities:
❑ You look away for a moment
❑ You turn your head
❑ You close your eyes
❑ Your face shows me you're about to cry
❑ Other ....

Your
ten typicals

These ten things are so typically you:

1 ....

2 ....

3 ....

4 ....

5 ....

6 ....

7 ....

8 ....

9 ....

10 ....

Your
firsts

There's a first for everything, and during this leap, these were your firsts:

First ....
....
....
....

First ....
....
....
....

First ....
....
....
....

First ....
....
....
....

First ....
....
....
....

First ....
....
....
....

Your
mighty milestones

My personal top 5 of all the developmental milestones you achieved are:

Milestone 1 ....

....

....

....

Milestone 2...

....

....

....

Milestone 3...

....

....

....

Milestone 4...

....

....

....

Milestone 5...

....

....

....

Date of your first real social smile: ....

Date of your first real tear: ....

(Y)our
special memory moments

....
....
....
....

....
....
....
....

....
....
....
....

....
....
....
....

...with pics to go along!

Your
typical yous

These are the nicknames I call you:

....
....
....
....

In our long chats, or better said my long monologues, I tell you:

....
....
....
....

This is what I learned from you:

....
....
....
....

These words describe you and your character best now:

....
....
....
....

Most beautiful/ awesome/ humorous comment someone made about you:

....
....
....
....

(Y)our
first letter (from me!)

Dear ....

....

....

....

....

....

....

....

....

....

....

....

....

....

....

....

....

....

....

....

....

....

Your handprint:

Date: ....
Weight: ....
Height: ....
Size: ....

Your
leaply scrapbook

Here you can keep all
your special memorabilia,
including receipts, tickets,
cards, drawings, little notes,
and photos!

The more, the better!
Collect and create
the best of each leap

My
notes

The World of
Patterns

Patterns are everywhere. You can
see, hear, feel, and even make them.

This
Wonder Week's fussy signs

Date: ....

You are now making your second leap. I noticed this because you:

....

....

....

On a scale of fussiness, I would say this leap is a:

☀— 1   2   3   4   5   6   7   8   9   10 ⛈

The top three ways to soothe you were:

1. ....

2. ....

3. ....

This is how I felt:

....

....

....

On a scale of feeling ❏ desperate / ❏ insecure / ❏ .... I felt:

☀— 1   2   3   4   5   6   7   8   9   10 ⛈

My cuddle care for you consists of:

....

....

Your
three C's

The difference in:

Clinginess:

....

....

Crying:

....

....

Crankiness:

....

....

And don't forget about the difference in:
Sleeping:

....

....

Drinking:

....

....

You...
- ❏ wanted more attention
- ❏ became shy with strangers
- ❏ clung to me more tightly
- ❏ slept poorly
- ❏ cried, cried, and cried some more

Yep, all this because progress is on its way. This leap made you perceive patterns for the first time in your life. The following pages are all about your exploration of the world of Patterns.

$\mathcal{Y}$our
exploration

It's clear that you perceive the world in a different way than before the leap.
This is what I noticed:

....

....

....

....

....

....

....

....

....

....

....

....

....

....

....

....

....

....

....

....

You now move in another way:

....

....

....

Your movements are a bit ❑ jerky/❑ rigid/❑ stiff/❑ like those of a puppet.

These are the things you are now able to do with your body:

....

....

....

With your hands you now:

....

....

....

You looked very closely and saw ....

These are the body parts you now discovered:

....

....

....

Your
love for visual patterns

Patterns are everywhere. Of all the patterns you saw around you, you love these the most:

....

....

....

....

....

....

....

....

....

....

....

....

....

....

....

....

Your
eyes

You now move and use your eyes in a different way:

....
....
....
....

When we go for a walk, you look at:

....
....
....
....

When you look at people, you like to look most at:

....
....
....
....

You now love to see...
❏ a flickering candle
❏ a waving curtain
❏ pets eating or moving
❏ people moving or eating
❏ bling, shiny clothing, or jewellery

Your
listening and chatting

You react to sounds differently now than before in a way that:

....

....

....

....

....

These are now the things you like to listen to:

....

....

....

....

....

These sounds scared you:

....

....

....

....

....

The short bursts of sounds you now are able to make sound like:

....

....

....

....

....

Your
play

Your most beloved toys are now:

....
....
....
....
....

These are the non-toy objects you like to "play" with or investigate at home:

....
....
....
....
....

And these are the non-toy objects you like to "play" with or investigate outside our home:

....
....
....
....
....

You prefer ❑ toys / ❑ "real things"

Your
special activities

Everybody has their own personal activities they like to do with you!

These things you like to do most with:

....

....

....

....

....

With .... your most loved activities are:

....

....

....

....

....

With .... you like to:

....

....

....

....

....

Your
gymnastics, songs, & faces

These real body gymnastic games you like best now are:

....
....
....
....

The songs I sing for you are:

....
....
....
....

Faces! I love these different faces you make:

....
....
....
....
....

Your first experiences

There's a first for everything, and during this leap, these were your firsts:

First ....
....
....
....

First ....
....
....
....

First ....
....
....
....

First ....
....
....
....

First ....
....
....
....

First ....
....
....
....

Your
mighty milestones

Milestone 1 ....
....
....
....

Milestone 2 ....
....
....
....

Milestone 3 ....
....
....
....

Milestone 4 ....
....
....
....

Milestone 5 ....
....
....
....

(Y)our
special memory moments

....
....
....
....

....
....
....
....

....
....
....
....

....
....
....
....

...with pics to go along!

Your
typical yous

In our long chats, or better said my long monologues, I tell you:

....
....
....
....

The difference now, though, is that you start to "talk" back. I'm pretty sure you're telling me :

....
....
....
....

This is what I learned from you:

....
....
....
....

These words describe you and your character best now:

....
....
....
....

Most beautiful/ awesome/ humorous comment someone made about you:

....
....
....
....

(Y)our
second letter (from me!)

Dear ....

....

....

....

....

....

....

....

....

....

....

....

....

....

....

....

....

....

....

....

....

Your handprint:

Date: ....

Weight: ....

Height: ....

Size: ....

Your leaply scrapbook

Cut out, stick, and keep all
your special memorabilia,
including receipts, tickets,
cards, drawings, little notes
and photos!

The more, the better!
Collect and create
the best of each leap

My notes

The World of
Smooth
Transitions

Something can become something
else in a smooth way such as the
dimming light or a sound from low to high.

This
Wonder Week's fussy signs

Date: ....

You are now making your third leap. I noticed this because you:

....
....
....

On a scale of fussiness, I would say this leap is a:

☼ 1   2   3   4   5   6   7   8   9   10 ⛈

The top three ways to soothe you were:

1. ....
2. ....
3. ....

This is how I felt:

....
....
....

On a scale of feeling ❏ desperate / ❏ insecure / ❏ .... I felt:

☼ 1   2   3   4   5   6   7   8   9   10 ⛈

Your
three C's

The difference in:

Clinginess:

....

....

Crying:

....

....

Crankiness:

....

....

And don't forget about the difference in:
Sleeping:

....

....

Drinking:

....

....

You...
- ❏ became shy with strangers
- ❏ clung to me more tightly
- ❏ lost your appetite
- ❏ slept poorly
- ❏ sucked your thumb more often
- ❏ were listless

Your
exploration

It's clear that you perceive the world in a different way than before the leap.
This is what I noticed:

....
....
....
....
....
....
....
....
....
....
....
....
....
....
....
....
....
....
....
....
....
....

Your
body control

You seem to have a different type of body control than before the leap. These are the main things I've noticed:

....
....
....
....

You move much more smoothly in this way:

....
....
....
....

The gymnastics and flexible tricks you perform with your body are:

....
....
....
....

Talking about "sitting," "rolling," and "holding" your head straight:

....
....
....
....

Your hands & touches

Only a few weeks ago, you discovered these two things we call hands.

Already, you now:

....

....

....

These are the things you like to do most with your hands:

....

....

....

If you touch my face, you:

....

....

....

If you touch your own face, you:

....

....

....

Your
eyes

You can now follow something with your eyes in a smooth way. This is a close-up picture of your eyes looking at your: ....

When you look at my face, you now look at:

....

....

....

....

You like to see the following smooth transitions around you:
- ❏ Lights being dimmed
- ❏ A hand going up
- ❏ A head being turned
- ❏ The smooth transitions in a toy
- ❏ Other ....

Your
emotions

You express your enjoyment through:
- ❏ Watching / Looking
- ❏ Listening
- ❏ Grabbing
- ❏ Talking then waiting for a response
- ❏ Other ....

You express different behaviour around different people. What I noticed:

....
....
....
....

You show me you're bored by:

....
....
....
....

Other new emotions I noticed were:

....
....
....
....

Your chats

You like to ❑ shriek / ❑ gurgle / ❑ make vowel-like sounds now all in a much smoother way than before the leap. These are the sounds you now make and when and where you do this:

....
....
....
....

If I imitate your sounds, you:

....
....
....
....

This is what I told you when we were chatting:

....
....
....
....

Your laugh tells my I've struck the right chord. This is what made you laugh this leap:

....
....
....
....

Your play

Your most beloved toys are now:

....
....
....

These are the non-toy objects you like to "play" with or investigate:

....
....
....

You started to explore the world by feeling all sorts of things:

....
....
....

This is the music you like most now:

....
....
....

I noticed this because this music makes you:

....
....
....

Your special activities

Just to give you an update of the games and things you do with whom:

These things you like to do most with:

....
....
....
....
....

With .... your most loved activities are:

....
....
....
....
....

With .... you like to:

....
....
....
....
....

Your firsts

There's a first for everything, and during this leap, these were your firsts:

First ....
....
....
....

First ....
....
....
....

First ....
....
....
....

First ....
....
....
....

First ....
....
....
....

First ....
....
....
....

Your mighty milestones

Milestone 1 ....
....
....
....

Milestone 2...
....
....
....

Milestone 3...
....
....
....

Milestone 4...
....
....
....

Milestone 5...
....
....
....

(Y)our
special memory moments

....
....
....
....

....
....
....
....

....
....
....
....

....
....
....
....

...with pics to go along!

Your
typical yous

This is what I learned from you:

....
....
....
....

Looking back over a trimester of being together with you:

....
....
....
....

These words describe you and your character best now:

....
....
....
....

Most beautiful/ awesome/ humorous comment someone made about you:

....
....
....
....

(Y)our third letter (from me!)

Dear ....

....

....

....

....

....

....

....

....

....

....

....

....

....

....

....

....

....

....

....

....

....

....

....

....

....

....

Your
leap is made!

Your handprint:

Date: ....

Weight: ....

Height: ....

Size: ....

Your
leaply scrapbook

Cut out, stick, and keep all
your special memorabilia,
including receipts, tickets,
cards, drawings, little notes,
and photos!

The more, the better!
Collect and create
the best of each leap

My notes

The World of
Events

Y ou got it! Two smooth
transitions or patterns
can actually be one event!

This
Wonder Week's fussy signs

Date: ....

You are now making your fourth leap. I noticed this because you:

....

....

....

On a scale of fussiness, I would say this leap is a:

☼ 1 2 3 4 5 6 7 8 9 10 ⚡

The top three ways to soothe you were:

1. ....

2. ....

3. ....

This is how I felt:

....

....

....

On a scale of feeling ❑ desperate / ❑ insecure / ❑ .... I felt:

☼ 1 2 3 4 5 6 7 8 9 10 ⚡

$\mathcal{Y}$our
three C's

The difference in:

Clinginess:

....

....

Crying:

....

....

Crankiness:

....

....

And don't forget about the difference in:
Sleeping:

....

....

Drinking:

....

....

You...
- ❑ had trouble sleeping
- ❑ became shy with strangers
- ❑ demanded more attention
- ❑ needed more head support
- ❑ wanted to always be with me
- ❑ lost your appetite
- ❑ were moody
- ❑ were listless

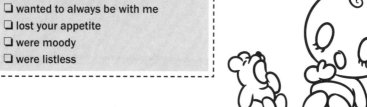

Your
exploration

It's clear that you perceive the world in a different way than before the leap. This is what I noticed:

....
....
....
....
....
....
....
....
....
....
....
....
....
....
....
....
....
....
....
....
....

Your
way of examining

You are now able to make several flowing movements in succession.

As a result you:

❑ reach for

❑ grab

❑ pull

toys towards you in one smooth movement to examine it.

You like to examine things by:

❑ Shaking

❑ Banging

❑ Poking

❑ Turning them around

❑ Sliding things up and down

❑ Putting the extra interesting things in your mouth

This is what and how you did this:

....

....

....

....

You feel with your mouth!

This is what you examined with your mouth:

....

....

....

....

Your observations

Sometimes you like to observe me doing things. For example:

....
....
....
....

Sometimes you body is too tired to continue the examination.
I then help you by:

....
....
....
....

There are certain details of object that interest you to the max. These are:

....
....
....
....

Your most loved materials are:

....
....
....
....

Your
sight & seeing

From all the daily chores, you like to watch:

....
....
....
....

Books... You're not reading them, but if I show you a colourful image on a page, you:..

If you look in the mirror or see me in the mirror, you:

....
....
....
....

These repetitive activities (i.e. jumping up and down, seeing someone brush his/her hair, or cutting bread) fascinate you most:

....
....
....
....

Your chatting and listening

You are now able to make real babbling sentences. Lately you told me:

....
....
....
....
....

The sound you like most is:

....
....
....
....
....

You now experiment with intonations and volume:

....
....
....
....
....

When someone says your name, you:

....
....
....
....

When you hear music you like, you:

....
....
....
....

You are now able to make "events" with your voice using both your lips and tongue. These new sounds are:

- ❏ Ffft-ffft-ffft
- ❏ Vvvv
- ❏ Zzz
- ❏ Sss
- ❏ Brrrr
- ❏ Arrrr
- ❏ Rrrr
- ❏ Grrr
- ❏ Prrr

Even when you yawn, you make noises. When you hear these noises, you:

....
....
....
....

If you cough and I answer by "coughing back," you:

....
....
....
....

Your body control & movements

These are the movement you now made and couldn't make before this leap:

....
....
....
....

You "ask" me to pick you by:

....
....
....
....

When I put you on the floor, you start to move:

....
....
....
....

You're now able to:
❑ Pass things from one hand to another
❑ Grab something if your hand comes in contact with it even without looking at it
❑ Grab things with either hand
❑ Shake a plaything
❑ Bang a plaything on a tabletop
❑ Deliberately throw things on the floor

Your
mouth & eating

When you had enough to eat, you:

....
....
....
....

If you see food or drinks or if you are hungry, you:

....
....
....
....

My mouth now seems really interesting to:

....
....
....
....

With your tongue, you now:

....
....
....
....

$\mathcal{Y}$our
special activities

Everybody has their own personal activities they love to do with you!

These things you like to do most with:

....

....

....

....

....

With .... your most loved activities are:

....

....

....

....

....

With .... you like to:

....

....

....

....

....

Your
games & toys

(& household things you see as toys)

When you're taking your bath, you like to play with:

....

....

....

....

When you're lying under or sitting next to an activity centre, you:

....

....

....

....

The toys you love most now and what you like to do with them:

....

....

....

....

When I tickle you, you:

....

....

....

....

firsts

There's a first for everything, and during this leap, these were your firsts:

First ....
....
....
....

First ....
....
....
....

First ....
....
....
....

First ....
....
....
....

First ....
....
....
....

First ....
....
....
....

Your mighty milestones

Milestone 1 ....
....
....
....

Milestone 2...
....
....
....

Milestone 3...
....
....
....

Milestone 4...
....
....
....

Milestone 5...
....
....
....

....

....

....

....

....

....

....

....

....

....

....

....

....

....

....

...with pics to go along!

....

....

....

....

....

....

....

....

....

....

This is what I learned from you:

....

....

....

....

....

Most beautiful/ awesome/ humorous comment someone made about you:

....

....

....

....

....

(Y)our
fourth letter (from me!)

Dear ....
....
....
....
....
....
....
....
....
....
....
....
....
....
....
....
....
....
....
....
....
....
....
....
....
....
....
....
....

Your leap is made!

Your handprint:

Date: ....
Weight: ....
Height: ....
Size: ....

Your
leaply scrapbook

Cut out, stick, and keep all
your special memorabilia,
including receipts, tickets,
cards, drawings, little notes,
and photos!

The more, the better!
Collect and create
the best of each leap

My notes

The world of
Relationships

Y ou understand the concepts of in, out,
behind, in front of, distances,
and the discovery that something
can be there but not visible to your
cute, little eyes.

This
Wonder Week's fussy signs

Date: ....

You are now making your fifth leap. I noticed this because you:

....

....

....

On a scale of fussiness, I would say this leap is a:

☼— 1   2   3   4   5   6   7   8   9   10 ⛈

The top three ways to soothe you were:

1. ....

2. ....

3. ....

This is how I felt:

....

....

....

On a scale of feeling ❑ desperate / ❑ insecure / ❑ .... I felt:

☼— 1   2   3   4   5   6   7   8   9   10 ⛈

Your
three C's

The difference in:

Clinginess:

....

....

Crying:

....

....

Crankiness:

....

....

And don't forget about the difference in:

Sleeping:

....

....

Drinking:

....

....

You...
- ❏ want me to keep you busy
- ❏ had "nightmares"
- ❏ lost your appetite
- ❏ are quieter and less vocal
- ❏ always wanted to be with me
- ❏ don't want me to change your diaper
- ❏ reached for cuddly objects more often
- ❏ were listless

Your exploration

It's clear that you perceive the world in a different way than before the leap. This is what I noticed:

....

....

....

....

....

....

....

....

....

....

....

....

....

....

....

....

....

....

....

....

....

Your
distance exploring

In, out, in front, behind, and next to are all keywords belonging to the leap of relationships. This is how I noticed you experimenting with these concepts:

....
....
....
....

The two things you like most to put in and out of each other are:

....
....
....
....

I've seen you studying the concept of distance by:

....
....
....
....

If I walk away and enlarge the distance between us, you:

....
....
....
....

Your actions result in

And you love experimenting with that.

You discovered these buttons and switches to flip:

....

....

You now realize things can be "taken apart," which is also a(n) (ex...) relationship between things. This is what you took apart:

....

....

You are tremendously interesed in examining little things like:
- ❏ Buttons
- ❏ Zippers
- ❏ Labels
- ❏ Stickers
- ❏ Marks on the wall
- ❏ Screws
- ❏ Other: ....

....

This is a picture of you playing with a little detail:

Your
body

This is the way you now use your hands to grab:

....
....
....
....
....

I've seen you lifting .... to look under it. You saw:

....
....
....
....
....

I've seen you mimicking these gestures:

....
....
....
....
....

If you get your hands on a ball, you:

....
....
....
....
....

Your
sight & seeing

When you observe adults, you like to look at:

....
....
....
....

The animal you like to watch most is:

....
....
....
....

I can see you looking from one thing to another:

....
....
....
....
....
....
....
....

Your smile

If somebody moves unusually, you:

....
....
....

When I coincidentally let something fall on the ground, you:

....
....
....

You laugh really hard when you see:

....
....
....
....
....
....
....
....
....
....
....
....

Your
chatting & listening

When you hear music, your body:

....
....
....
....

You made the connections between the meaning of little sentences and the words! I can see you understand:
❏ No, don't do that
❏ Come on, let's go
❏ Others:

....
....
....
....

When you hear voices or sounds coming out my phone, you:

....
....
....
....

You are trying to say words. Sometimes, I think I can almost make out that you are trying to say:

....
....
....

Your
first six months

You're my mini-me in the way that:

....
....
....
....
....
....
....
....
....
....
....
....
....
....
....
....

months

Your
special activities

Everybody has their own personal activities they like to do with you!

These things you like to do most with:

....

....

....

....

....

With .... your most loved activities are:

....

....

....

....

....

With .... you like to:

....

....

....

....

....

Your games & toys

(& household things you see as toys)

When you're taking your bath, you like to play with:

....
....
....
....
....
....
....
....
....
....
....
....
....
....
....
....
....
....
....
....
....

Your
firsts

There's a first for everything, and during this leap, these were your firsts:

First ....
....
....
....

First ....
....
....
....

First ....
....
....
....

First ....
....
....
....

First ....
....
....
....

First ....
....
....
....

Your **mighty milestones**

Milestone 1 ....

....

....

....

Milestone 2..

....

....

....

Milestone 3..

....

....

....

Milestone 4..

....

....

....

Milestone 5..

....

....

....

(Y)our
special memory moments

....
....
....
....
....

....
....
....
....
....

....
....
....
....
....

...with pics to go along!

....
....
....
....
....

....
....
....
....
....

This is what I learned from you:

....
....
....
....
....

Most beautiful/ awesome/ humorous comment someone made about you:

....
....
....
....
....

(Y)our
fifth letter (from me!)

Dear ....

....

....

....

....

....

....

....

....

....

....

....

....

....

....

....

....

....

....

....

....

....

....

....

....

....

....

Your leap is made!

Your handprint:

Date: ....

Weight: ....

Height: ....

Size: ....

Your leaply scrapbook

Cut out, stick, and keep all
your special memorabilia,
including receipts, tickets,
cards, drawings, little notes,
and photos!

The more, the better!
Collect and create
the best of each leap

My notes

The World of
Categories

𝒴ou can divide the world into
all kinds of categories.

This
Wonder Week's fussy signs

Date: ....

You are now making your sixth leap. I noticed this because you:

....

....

....

On a scale of fussiness, I would say this leap is a:

☀ 1 2 3 4 5 6 7 8 9 10 ⛈

The top three ways to soothe you were:

1. ....

2. ....

3. ....

This is how I felt:

....

....

....

On a scale of feeling ❏ desperate / ❏ insecure / ❏ .... I felt:

☀ 1 2 3 4 5 6 7 8 9 10 ⛈

Your
three C's

The difference in:

Clinginess:

....

....

Crying:

....

....

Crankiness:

....

....

And don't forget about the difference in:

Sleeping:

....

....

Drinking:

....

....

You...
- ❏ clung to my clothes
- ❏ were shy
- ❏ held on to me tightly
- ❏ demanded more attention
- ❏ had "nightmares"
- ❏ acted extra sweet
- ❏ were listless
- ❏ refused to get your diaper changed
- ❏ babbled less
- ❏ were less lively

Your exploration

It's clear that you perceive the world in a different way than before the leap. This is what I noticed:

....
....
....
....
....
....
....
....
....
....
....
....
....
....
....
....
....
....
....
....
....
....

Your recollection of

You showed that you could recognize a specific animal or person by:

....

....

....

....

....

When I ask you where the .... is in the book, you point it out!

You know when something is dirty. You show this by:

....

....

....

....

....

You recognize and imitate expressions and movements of people:

....

....

....

....

....

Your emotions

When you look in the mirror, you:

....
....
....
....

If I pay attention to someone else, you:

....
....
....
....

When your teddy falls, you:

....
....
....
....

When you hear another child crying, you:

....
....
....
....

Your
try-outs

You try to switch roles by:

❏ Playing peek-a-boo with a younger baby

❏ Feeding the bottle to me

❏ Inviting me to sing a song and then start clapping your hands

❏ Handing me the blocks to build a tower

❏ Other: ....

This is a story about the first time you showed me you wanted to switch roles:

....

....

....

....

....

....

....

....

....

....

....

Your exploring by investigation

Categories are groups of things with the same characteristics. And you already start to explore these categories and characteristics now.

Categories you were investigating with your toys:

....
....
....
....
....
....
....
....

Categories you were investigating in humans:

....
....
....
....
....
....
....
....

Categories you were investigating outside:

....
....
....
....
....
....
....

Categories you were investigating in our house:

....
....
....
....
....
....
....

You explored categories like stickiness/ roughness / warmth / slipperiness by:

....
....
....
....
....
....
....

Your
chatting & laughing

You have a different sound-word for everybody in our family.

Here's how you call everybody:

....
....
....
....
....

The words I'm sure you now really understand are:

....
....
....
....
....

What made you laugh most was:

....
....
....
....
....

Your
examinations

Inside, you love to examine:

....
....
....
....

Outside, you love to examine:

....
....
....
....

With .... you like to examine:

....
....
....
....

In terms of demolition, you like to examine:

....
....
....
....

Your
special activities

These things you like to do most with:

....

....

....

....

....

....

With .... your most loved activities are:

....

....

....

....

....

....

With .... you like to:

....

....

....

....

....

Your
games & toys

A magazine or newspaper to you is:

....
....
....

If you see handles or knobs, you:

....
....
....

The game that you absolutely adore is:

....
....
....

These are now your most loved toys and what you like to do with them:

....
....
....

When I tickle you, you:

....
....
....

There's a first for everything, and during this leap, these were your firsts:

First ....
....
....
....

First ....
....
....
....

First ....
....
....
....

First ....
....
....
....

First ....
....
....
....

First ....
....
....
....

Your
mighty milestones

Milestone 1 ....
....
....
....

Milestone 2..
....
....
....

Milestone 3..
....
....
....

Milestone 4..
....
....
....

Milestone 5..
....
....
....

(Y)our
special memory moments

....
....
....
....
....

....
....
....
....
....

....
....
....
....
....

...with pics to go along!

....

....

....

....

....

....

....

....

....

....

....

This is what I learned from you:

....

....

....

....

....

Most beautiful/ awesome/ humorous comment someone made about you:

....

....

....

....

....

(Y)our
sixth letter (from me!)

Dear ....

....

....

....

....

....

....

....

....

....

....

....

....

....

....

....

....

....

....

....

....

....

Your handprint:

Date: ....

Weight: ....

Height: ....

Size: ....

Your leaply scrapbook

Cut out, stick, and keep all
your special memorabilia,
including receipts, tickets,
cards, drawings, little notes,
and photos!

The more, the better!
Collect and create
the best of each leap

My notes

The World of
Sequences

N ow, you can do two things in
a row that lead up to one big goal.

This
Wonder Week's fussy signs

Date: ....

You are now making your seventh leap. I noticed this because you:

....
....
....

On a scale of fussiness, I would say this leap is a:

☼– 1   2   3   4   5   6   7   8   9   10 ⚡

The top three ways to soothe you were:

1. ....
2. ....
3. ....

This is how I felt:

....
....
....

On a scale of feeling ❑ desperate / ❑ insecure / ❑ .... I felt:

☼– 1   2   3   4   5   6   7   8   9   10 ⚡

My cuddle care for you consists of:

....
....

Your
three C's

The difference in:

Clinginess:

....

....

Crying:

....

....

Crankiness:

....

....

And don't forget about the difference in:

Sleeping:

....

....

Drinking:

....

....

You...
- ❑ were shy with others
- ❑ wanted to be kept busy
- ❑ were jealous
- ❑ were listless
- ❑ refused to get your diaper changed
- ❑ lost you appetite
- ❑ behaved more babyish
- ❑ acted unusually sweet
- ❑ were cheerful one moment, crying the next
- ❑ babbled less
- ❑ sat there, quietly dreaming
- ❑ sucked your thumb more often
- ❑ cuddled toys more often

Your exploration

It's clear that you perceive the world in a different way than before the leap.
This is what I noticed:

....
....
....
....
....
....
....
....
....
....
....
....
....
....
....
....
....
....
....

Your
pointing & talking

You try to get me to tell you the names of objects, people, and animals by:

....

....

....

When I say someone's name and that person is around, you:

....

....

....

If I ask you where your .... is, you:

....

....

....

These are the animals sounds you make when I ask you what this animals says:

....

....

....

These are the words or sounds you make now:

....

....

....

If I give you a key, you:

....
....
....
....
....

If I switch on the light, you:

....
....
....
....
....

If I put you in the sandpit with a small shovel, you:

....
....
....
....
....

If I give you blocks, you:

....
....
....
....
....

Your
tool-using, goal-reaching skills

When you try to get up or "walk" around, you:

....
....
....
....
....

If you can't reach something, you:

....
....
....
....
....

When you want me to take you in a specific direction, you:

....
....
....
....
....

Your
sequences

These are some example sequences you now did:

First you   **Then you**

....
....
....
....
....
....
....
....
....
....
....
....
....
....
....
....
....

You can't do three things in a row until you make your next leap. Sometimes
the outcome is hilarious. For example, when you:

....
....
....
....
....
....
....
....
....

I can see you imitating two gestures someone made:

....
....
....
....
....
....
....
....
....

The movements you copy when we sing a nursery rhyme:

....
....
....
....
....
....
....
....
....

Your construction

The first thing you constructed was:

....
....
....
....
....

The first time I saw you putting things together was:

....
....
....
....
....

I see you are linking things:

....
....
....
....
....

Your eating

These are the funny things you do when you eat:

....
....
....
....
....

You seem to want to share your food with:

....
....
....
....
....

You want ❏ me to feed you / ❏ to feed yourself.

If I give you a spoon and your food, you:

....
....
....
....
....

Your
special activities

Everybody has their own personal activities they like to do with you!

These things you like to do most with:

....

....

....

....

....

With .... your most loved activities are:

....

....

....

....

....

With .... you like to:

....

....

....

....

....

$\mathcal{Y}our$
games & toys
(& household things you see as toys)

Your most loved nursery rhyme: ....

When you hear it, you:

....

....

....

....

Your most loved toys are now:

....

....

....

....

After spending almost a year with you, I think these kinds of things appeal
most to your character:

....

....

....

....

Your firsts

There's a first for everything, and during this leap, these were your firsts:

First ....
....
....
....

First ....
....
....
....

First ....
....
....
....

First ....
....
....
....

First ....
....
....
....

First ....
....
....
....

Your
mighty milestones

Milestone 1 ....
....
....
....

Milestone 2 ....
....
....
....

Milestone 3 ....
....
....
....

Milestone 4 ....
....
....
....

Milestone 5 ....
....
....
....

(Y)our
special memory moments

....
....
....
....
....

....
....
....
....
....

...with pics to go along!

....

....

....

....

....

....

....

....

....

....

....

....

....

....

....

(Y)our
seventh letter (from me!)

Dear ....

....

....

....

....

....

....

....

....

....

....

....

....

....

....

....

....

....

....

....

....

....

....

....

Your
leap is made!

Your handprint:

Date: ....

Weight: ....

Height: ....

Size: ....

Your **leaply scrapbook**

Cut out, stick, or note all
your special memorabilia,
including tourist's, ticket
cards, drawings, notes
and photos!

The more, the better!
Collect and create
the best of each leap

My notes

One year

Happy first birthday!

One year

....
....
....

These people came to congratulate you on your very first birthday:

....

....

....

....

....

These are the presents that you received:

....

....

....

....

....

This is what you did on your day in the spotlight:

....

....

....

....

....

My
notes

The World of
Programs

You understand our daily programs
and even participate
in your own way.

This
Wonder Week's fussy signs

Date: ....

You are now making your eighth leap. I noticed this because you:

....

....

....

On a scale of fussiness, I would say this leap is a:

☼ — 1   2   3   4   5   6   7   8   9   10 ⛈

The top three ways to soothe you were:

1. ....

2. ....

3. ....

This is how I felt:

....

....

....

On a scale of feeling ❑ desperate / ❑ insecure / ❑ .... I felt:

☼ — 1   2   3   4   5   6   7   8   9   10 ⛈

Your
three C's

The difference in:

Clinginess:

....

....

Crying:

....

....

Crankiness:

....

....

And don't forget about the difference in:

Sleeping:

....

....

Drinking:

....

....

You...
- ❑ were shyer with strangers
- ❑ wanted to be entertained more
- ❑ were jealous
- ❑ slept poorly
- ❑ were "daydreaming"
- ❑ behaved more babyish
- ❑ acted unusually sweet
- ❑ had more temper tantrums
- ❑ were mischievous
- ❑ sucked your thumb more often

Your
exploration

It's clear that you perceive the world in a different way than before the leap.
This is what I noticed:

....

....

....

....

....

....

....

....

....

....

....

....

....

....

....

....

....

....

....

....

....

....

Your
initiatives of programs

You showed me you wanted to .... by:

....

....

....

....

....

You sometimes try to help out in the house by:

....

....

....

....

....

You show me you want a treat by:

....

....

....

....

....

Your
help & love for the should-be

You really know how things "should be done," and if they're not done this way, you correct it.

❑ (Tried) hanging the towel were it should hang
❑ (Tried) putting something in the right cupboard
❑ Came to me with things you wanted to be put away
❑ Got a shovel and was ready to go to the sandpit

Other programs you "corrected:"

....
....
....
....
....

You tried to help me by:

....
....
....
....
....

Your
independent programs

Feeding your toys, bathing a doll, eating raisins out of a package without help, and building a tower of at least three blocks are all examples of programs. These are the programs you did!

Program 1:

....
....
....
....
....

Program 2:

....
....
....
....
....

Program 3:

....
....
....
....
....

$\mathcal{Y}$our
independence

If I let you try to eat on your own, you:

....

....

....

....

If you get your hands on my phone, you:

....

....

....

....

If we get dressed, you:

....

....

....

....

When you think it's time for dessert, you:

....

....

....

....

Your
language & music

You now like to listen to........ minute stories
preferably on ❑ TV/ ❑ in a book / ❑ both

Your most loved story is about: ....

When you "tell" a story, you use (the sounds of):
❑ Questions
❑ Exclamations
❑ Pauses
❑ Different voices
❑ Low-high effects

The words you now say are:
....
....
....

The music you love most:
....
....
....

The instrument you like to play:
....
....
....

Your emotions

You were afraid of:

....

....

....

....

....

If you see someone is sad, you:

....

....

....

....

....

This is what made you laugh really loud:

....

....

....

....

....

Your
exploration of
the world outside

❑ You like to go outside / ❑ You're more the stay-at-home type.

If we go outside, you love to:

....
....
....
....

When grocery shopping, you:

....
....
....
....

You like to ❑ be carried / ❑ ride in the stroller / ❑ try to walk.

The things you discovered outside that you loved the most during this leap
are:

....
....
....
....

Your special activities

These things you like to do most with:

....
....
....
....
....

With .... your most loved activities are:

....
....
....
....
....

With .... you like to:

....
....
....
....
....

Your
games & toys

(& household things you see as toys)

When I give you a pen and some paper, you:

....
....
....
....

To you, a book is:

....
....
....
....

Your most loved toys now are:

....
....
....
....

Your most loved activities are:

....
....
....
....

There's a first for everything, and during this leap, these were your firsts:

First ....
....
....
....

First ....
....
....
....

First ....
....
....
....

First ....
....
....
....

First ....
....
....
....

First ....
....
....
....

Your mighty milestones

Milestone 1 ....
....
....
....
....

Milestone 2...
....
....
....
....

Milestone 3...
....
....
....
....

Milestone 4...
....
....
....
....

Milestone 5...
....
....
....
....

...with pics to go along!

....

....

....

....

....

....

....

....

....

....

....

This is what I learned from you:

....

....

....

....

....

Most beautiful/ awesome/ humorous comment someone made about you:

....

....

....

....

....

(Y)our eighth letter (from me!)

Dear ....

....

....

....

....

....

....

....

....

....

....

....

....

....

....

....

....

....

....

....

....

....

Your leap is made!

Your handprint:

Date: ....

Weight: ....

Height: ....

Size: ....

Your leaply scrapbook

Cut out, stick, and keep all
your special memorabilia,
including receipts, tickets,
cards, drawings, little notes,
and photos!

The more, the better!
Collect and create
the best of each leap

My notes

The world of
Principles

A n artist is born and
so is the hunger for rules.

This
Wonder Week's fussy signs

Date: ....

You are now making your ninth leap. I noticed this because you:

....

....

....

On a scale of fussiness, I would say this leap is a:

☀ — 1   2   3   4   5   6   7   8   9   10 ⛈

The top three ways to soothe you were:

1. ....

2. ....

3. ....

This is how I felt:

....

....

....

On a scale of feeling ❑ desperate / ❑ insecure / ❑ .... I felt:

☀ — 1   2   3   4   5   6   7   8   9   10 ⛈

Your three C's

The difference in:

Clinginess:

....

....

Crying:

....

....

Crankiness:

....

....

And don't forget about the difference in:

Sleeping:

....

....

Drinking:

....

....

You...
- ❏ were more irritable
- ❏ were more impatient
- ❏ were more frustrated
- ❏ got angry more often
- ❏ rarely laughed anymore
- ❏ were sad more often
- ❏ wanted to be entertained more often
- ❏ daydreamed a lot
- ❏ had nightmares
- ❏ cuddled me or cuddled more often
- ❏ had more temper tantrums

Your
exploration

It's clear that you perceive the world in a different way than before the leap. This is what I noticed:

....
....
....
....
....
....
....
....
....
....
....
....
....
....
....
....
....
....
....

Your
choices

You are now able to choose what or how to do something. I've seen you:

Thinking:
- ❏ Should I wreck the tower or not?
- ❏ Should I continue playing with the blocks or switch to the doll?
- ❏ Should I do it this way or that way?
- ❏ Should I ask dad or grandma to get me a candy?
- ❏ What is the best strategy to keep me out of bed longest?

Other choices I've seen you making are:

....

....

....

....

....

....

....

....

....

....

....

....

....

Your
strategies & how-tos

I've also seen you playing with how-tos.

Things you did extremely carefully:

....
....
....
....
....

Things you did purposefully and recklessly:

....
....
....
....
....

Other strategies you've tried out:

....
....
....
....
....

Your
changes

I noticed that you think differently:

....
....
....
....

You handle toys differently:

....
....
....
....

Your sense of humour has changed:

....
....
....
....

Your toddlerhood

These are the biggest differences I see between this phase and the baby phase:

Baby phase   Toddler phase

....
....
....
....
....
....
....
....
....
....
....
....
....
....

Your
toddler temper tantrums

Date: ....

Location: ....

Why you threw a temper tantrum:

....

....

....

....

How you did it:

....

....

....

....

How I felt:

....

....

....

....

After it was over:

....

....

....

....

Your
skills

Exercising your own will:

❑ Chooses consciously

❑ Takes initiative

❑ Wants to give input if others do something

❑ Feels the need to belong/ be accepted

❑ Possessive with toys

Copying and imitating:

❑ Observes adults

❑ Observes other children

❑ Imitates sweet behaviour

❑ Imitates aggressive behaviour

❑ Imitates physical actions (i.e. somersault, climbing, etc.)

❑ Imitates subtle motor skills (i.e. holding a pencil)

❑ Imitates "oddities" (i.e. limping, walking like a hunchback, etc.)

❑ Imitates things on TV or in a book

Experiments with:

❏ Motor skills

❏ Stashing and recovering objects

❏ Crawling in or behind something and getting out again

❏ Manipulating things with caution and care

❏ Making choices: what shall I choose?

❏ The meaning of "yes" and "no"

❏ Fooling mom: acts like he/she is disobedient

❏ Ramps and rises: feels with his/her finger and studies them or runs
   his/her cars up and down them.

Implementing strategies:

❏ Is helpful (more often) or tries to be

❏ Is obedient (more often), careful, and caring or tries to be

❏ Accepts (more often) that he/she is still small

❏ Makes fun to get something or to get others to do something

❏ Is (more often) extra sweet to get his/her way

❏ Tries to get his/her way by being pushy

❏ Shows (more often) what he/she feels like/goes his/her own way

❏ Makes use of others to get something done

Your
special activities

These things you like to do most with:

....
....
....
....
....
....

With .... your most loved activities are:

....
....
....
....
....
....

With .... you like to:

....
....
....
....
....
....

Your
love for

When we read a book:

....
....
....

Your most loved toys now are:

....
....
....

Your most loved activities are:

....
....
....

Your most loved songs are:

....
....
....

There's a first for everything, and during this leap, these were your firsts:

First ....
....
....
....

First ....
....
....
....

First ....
....
....
....

First ....
....
....
....

First ....
....
....
....

First ....
....
....
....

Your
mighty milestones

Milestone 1 ....
....
....
....

Milestone 2 ....
....
....
....

Milestone 3 ....
....
....
....

Milestone 4 ....
....
....
....

Milestone 5 ....
....
....
....

(Y)our
special memory moments

....
....
....
....

....
....
....
....

....
....
....
....

....
....
....
....

...with pics to go along!

Your
typical yous

These are the nicknames I call you:

....

....

....

This is what I learned from you:

....

....

....

This is the funniest thing you did / said:

....

....

....

Most beautiful/ awesome/ humorous comment someone made about you:

....

....

....

(Y)our
ninth letter (from me!)

Dear ....

....

....

....

....

....

....

....

....

....

....

....

....

....

....

....

....

....

....

....

....

....

Your leap is made!

Your handprint:

Date: ....

Weight: ....

Height: ....

Size: ....

Your leaply scrapbook

Cut out, stick, and keep all
your special memorabilia,
including receipts, tickets,
cards, drawings, little notes,
and photos!

The more, the better!
Collect and create
the best of each leap

My notes

The World of Systems

Your last toddler leap.

This
Wonder Week's fussy signs

Date: ....

You are now making your last leap. I noticed this because you:

....
....
....

On a scale of fussiness, I would say this leap is a:

☼ — 1   2   3   4   5   6   7   8   9   10 ⛈

The top three ways to soothe you were:

1. ....
2. ....
3. ....

This is how I felt:

....
....
....

On a scale of feeling ❏ desperate / ❏ insecure / ❏ .... I felt:

☼ — 1   2   3   4   5   6   7   8   9   10 ⛈

Your
three C's

The difference in:

Clinginess:

....
....

Crying:

....
....

Crankiness:

....
....

And don't forget about the difference in:

Sleeping:

....
....

Drinking:

....
....

You...
- ❏ were cheerful one moment, crying the next
- ❏ wanted to be more entertained
- ❏ acted unusually sweet
- ❏ were mischievous
- ❏ threw more temper tantrums
- ❏ were jealous
- ❏ had nightmares
- ❏ were daydreaming
- ❏ were more babyish

Your
exploration

It's clear that you perceive the world in a different way than before the leap.
This is what I noticed:

....

....

....

....

....

....

....

....

....

....

....

....

....

....

....

....

....

....

....

....

Your
conscience

When I see you doing something you know you're not allowed, you:

....
....
....
....
....

Sometimes you test me out by:

....
....
....
....
....

You are able to "lie:"

....
....
....
....
....

Your
notion of self

These are the things you can now do all on you own:

....
....
....

You have your own will:

....
....
....

You can decide for yourself:

....
....
....

You want power:

....
....
....

Your
notion of you and others

You show me that things out of sight but are not out of your mind by:

....

....

....

....

You are noticing the differences between you and others:

....

....

....

....

You now understand that another child can want something else, than you do:

....

....

....

....

You know exactly who belongs to whom:

....

....

....

....

Your
knowledge

You have a pretty good map in your head and know where everything is. You show me this by:

....
....
....
....

You know what belongs to whom, and you show me by:

....
....
....
....

You know how to make up games. This is your latest invention:

....
....
....
....

You are a master of art now. This is your latest piece:

Title:

....

Your language

Wow, you've learned a lot!

You now understand most of what is said. Lately, you:

....

....

....

....

Your most loved words are:

....

....

....

....

The funniest thing you said / did with sounds was:

....

....

....

....

Books are:

....

....

....

....

Your
sense of time

For the first time, I noticed you have remembered past experiences:

....

....

....

....

If I make you a promise, hours later you:

....

....

....

....

You are starting to plan things. Your latest plan was:

....

....

....

....

Your special activities

These things you like to do most with:

....
....
....
....
....
....

With .... your most loved activities are:

....
....
....
....
....
....

With .... you like to:

....
....
....
....
....
....

Your
fantasy

I noticed you now have a sense of imagination when I saw you:

....
....
....
....

The latest "joke" you made was:

....
....
....
....

Your most loved songs / toys / activities are:

....
....
....
....

Your firsts

There's a first for everything, and during this leap, these were your firsts:

First ....
....
....
....

First ....
....
....
....

First ....
....
....
....

First ....
....
....
....

First ....
....
....
....

First ....
....
....
....

Your
mighty milestones

Milestone 1 ....

....

....

....

Milestone 2...

....

....

....

Milestone 3...

....

....

....

Milestone 4...

....

....

....

Milestone 5...

....

....

....

(Y)our
special memory moments

....
....
....
....
....

....
....
....
....
....

....
....
....
....
....

...with pics to go along!

....
....
....
....
....

....
....
....
....
....

This is what I learned from you:

....
....
....
....

Most beautiful/ awesome/ humorous comment someone made about you:

....
....
....
....

(Y)our tenth letter (from me!)

Dear ....

....

....

....

....

....

....

....

....

....

....

....

....

....

....

....

....

....

....

....

....

....

....

....

Your handprint:

Date: ....
Weight: ....
Height: ....
Size: ....

Your leaply scrapbook

The more, the better!
Collect and create
the best of each leap

My
notes

**You made your
first ten magical leaps!**

This is a picture of you and me, forever and ever